HORN

101 CLASSICAL THEMES

Note: The keys in this book do not match the other wind instruments.

Available for
FLUTE, CLARINET, ALTO SAX, TENOR SAX, TRUMPET,
HORN, TROMBONE, VIOLIN, VIOLA, CELLO

ISBN 978-1-4950-5629-1

Hal•Leonard®
CORPORATION
7777 W. BLUEMOUND RD. P.O. BOX 13819 MILWAUKEE, WI 53213

In Australia Contact:
Hal Leonard Australia Pty. Ltd.
4 Lentara Court
Cheltenham, Victoria, 3192 Australia
Email: ausadmin@halleonard.com.au

Visit Hal Leonard Online at
www.halleonard.com

CONTENTS

1812 OVERTURE
(Theme)

HORN

PYOTR IL'YICH TCHAIKOVSKY

Allegro vivace

AIR
from WATER MUSIC

GEORGE FRIDERIC HANDEL

Andante

AIR ON THE G STRING
from ORCHESTRAL SUITE NO. 3

JOHANN SEBASTIAN BACH

ARIOSO
from CANTATA 156

HORN

JOHANN SEBASTIAN BACH

Adagio

AVE MARIA
based on "Prelude in C Major" by Johann Sebastian Bach

HORN

CHARLES GOUNOD

ANDANTE CANTABILE
from STRING QUARTET NO. 1

HORN

PYOTR IL'YICH TCHAIKOVSKY

AVE MARIA

FRANZ SCHUBERT

BIST DU BEI MIR

GOTTFRIED HEINRICH STÖZEL
(previously attributed to J.S. Bach)

AVE VERUM CORPUS

HORN

WOLFGANG AMADEUS MOZART

Adagio

BADINERIE
from ORCHESTRAL SUITE NO. 2

HORN

JOHANN SEBASTIAN BACH

BARCAROLLE
from THE TALES OF HOFFMANN

HORN

JACQUES OFFENBACH

Moderately

BLUE DANUBE WALTZ

HORN

JOHANN STRAUSS, JR.

BOURRÉE IN E MINOR
from LUTE SUITE IN E MINOR

HORN

JOHANN SEBASTIAN BACH

Lively

BRANDENBURG CONCERTO NO. 3
(First Movement Theme)

JOHANN SEBASTIAN BACH

Moderately

BRANDENBURG CONCERTO NO. 5

(First Movement Theme)

JOHANN SEBASTIAN BACH

Moderately

BRIDAL CHORUS
from LOHENGRIN

HORN

RICHARD WAGNER

CLAIR DE LUNE
from SUITE BERGAMASQUE

HORN

CLAUDE DEBUSSY

Andante

CAN CAN
from ORPHEUS IN THE UNDERWORLD

HORN

JACQUES OFFENBACH

Allegretto moderato

CANON IN D

JOHANN PACHELBEL

Adagio

CARO MIO BEN

TOMMASO GIORDANI

Larghetto

DANCE OF THE HOURS

from LA GIOCONDA

HORN

AMILCARE PONCHIELLI

Moderately

DANCE OF THE REED-FLUTES

from THE NUTCRACKER

HORN

PYOTR IL'YICH TCHAIKOVSKY

DANCE OF THE SPIRITS
from ORFEO ED EURIDICE

HORN

CHRISTOPH WILLIBALD VON GLUCK

Andante

DANCE OF THE SUGAR PLUM FAIRY
from THE NUTCRACKER

PYOTR IL'YICH TCHAIKOVSKY

Andante ma non troppo

EINE KLEINE NACHTMUSIK

(First Movement Theme)

WOLFGANG AMADEUS MOZART

EVENING PRAYER
from HANSEL AND GRETEL

HORN

ENGELBERT HUMPERDINCK

Moderately

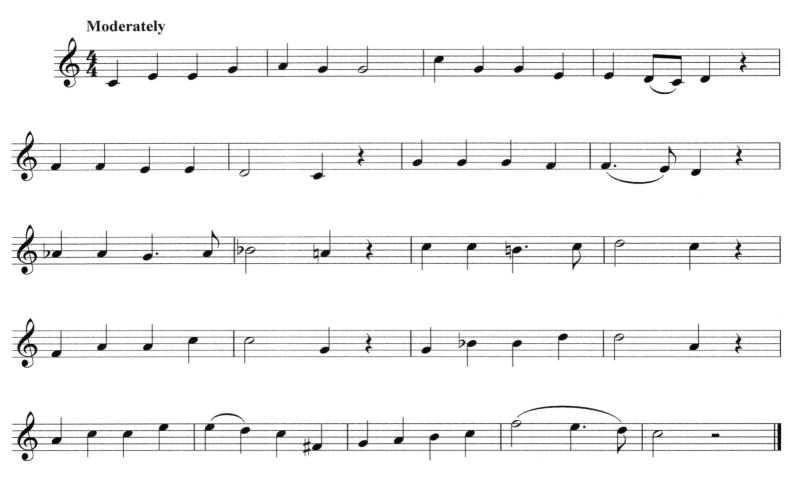

THE FLIGHT OF THE BUMBLEBEE

NICOLAI RIMSKY-KORSAKOV

Vivace

EINE KLEINE NACHTMUSIK

(Second Movement Theme: "Romanze")

HORN

WOLFGANG AMADEUS MOZART

FLOWER DUET

from LAKMÉ

HORN

LÉO DELIBES

Andantino con moto

FUNERAL MARCH
(Marche funèbre)
from PIANO SONATA NO. 2

HORN

FRÉDÉRIC CHOPIN

FUNERAL MARCH OF A MARIONETTE

HORN

CHARLES GOUNOD

Allegretto

FÜR ELISE
(Bagatelle No. 25)

HORN

LUDWIG VAN BEETHOVEN

THE GREAT GATE OF KIEV
from PICTURES AT AN EXHIBITION

MODEST MUSSORGSKY

Largo grandioso

GYMNOPÉDIE NO. 1

ERIC SATIE

Lent et douloureux

HABANERA
from CARMEN

HORN

GEORGES BIZET

Allegro quasi andantino

THE HAPPY FARMER
from ALBUM FOR THE YOUNG

HORN

ROBERT SCHUMANN

Brightly, cheerfully

THE HARMONIOUS BLACKSMITH
from HARPSICHORD SUITE NO. 5

GEORGE FRIDERIC HANDEL

Andante

HORNPIPE
from WATER MUSIC

HORN

GEORGE FRIDERIC HANDEL

Allegro maestoso

HUNGARIAN DANCE NO. 5

HORN

JOHANNES BRAHMS

Allegro

Slower

Tempo I

HALLELUJAH CHORUS
from MESSIAH

HORN

GEORGE FRIDERIC HANDEL

INTERMEZZO
from CAVALLERIA RUSTICANA

PIETRO MASCAGNI

JERUSALEM

HUBERT PARRY

IN THE HALL OF THE MOUNTAIN KING

from PEER GYNT

HORN

EDVARD GRIEG

JESU, JOY OF MAN'S DESIRING
from CANTATA 147

HORN

JOHANN SEBASTIAN BACH

Moderately

LARGO
from XERXES

HORN

GEORGE FRIDERIC HANDEL

Larghetto

LAUDATE DOMINUM
from VESPERAE SOLENNES DE CONFESSORE

HORN

WOLFGANG AMADEUS MOZART

LULLABY
(Wiegenlied)

HORN

JOHANNES BRAHMS

Moderately, tenderly

LIEBESTRAUM

FRANZ LISZT

Poco allegro

D.S. al Fine

MELODY IN F

ANTON RUBINSTEIN

Moderately

Fine

D.C. al Fine
(no repeat)

MARCH
from THE NUTCRACKER

HORN

PYOTR IL'YICH TCHAIKOVSKY

MARCHE SLAVE

HORN

PYOTR IL'YICH TCHAIKOVSKY

MINUET
from STRING QUINTET NO. 5

HORN

LUIGI BOCCHERINI

OVERTURE
from THE NUTCRACKER

HORN

PYOTR IL'YICH TCHAIKOVSKY

Allegro

MORNING
from PEER GYNT

HORN

EDVARD GRIEG

Allegretto pastorale

MINUET IN G
from ANNA MAGDALENA NOTEBOOK

JOHANN SEBASTIAN BACH

50

MINUET IN G

HORN

LUDWIG VAN BEETHOVEN

ODE TO JOY
from SYMPHONY NO. 9

LUDWIG VAN BEETHOVEN

PANIS ANGELICUS

CESAR FRANCK

PIANO SONATA NO. 8: "PATHÉTIQUE"
(Second Movement Theme)

HORN

LUDWIG VAN BEETHOVEN

Adagio cantabile

PIANO CONCERTO IN A MINOR
(First Movement Theme)

EDVARD GRIEG

Allegro

PIANO CONCERTO NO. 21
(Second Movement Theme)

WOLFGANG AMADEUS MOZART

Andante

PAVANE

HORN

GABRIEL FAURÉ

PIE JESU
from REQUIEM

HORN

GABRIEL FAURÉ

Adagio

PIANO SONATA IN C MAJOR
(First Movement Theme)

HORN

WOLFGANG AMADEUS MOZART

PRELUDE IN A MAJOR, OP. 28, NO. 7

FRÉDÉRIC CHOPIN

POLOVETZIAN DANCE
from PRINCE IGOR

HORN

ALEXANDER BORODIN

PRELUDE IN C MINOR, OP. 28, NO. 20

HORN

FRÉDÉRIC CHOPIN

SINFONIA
from CHRISTMAS ORATORIO

JOHANN SEBASTIAN BACH

ROMEO AND JULIET
(Love Theme)

HORN

PYOTR IL'YICH TCHAIKOVSKY

POMP AND CIRCUMSTANCE

HORN

EDWARD ELGAR

RONDEAU

JEAN-JOSEPH MOURET

RONDO ALLA TURCA
from PIANO SONATA NO. 11

WOLFGANG AMADEUS MOZART

SHEEP MAY SAFELY GRAZE

from CANTATA 208

HORN

JOHANN SEBASTIAN BACH

Moderately

THE SORCERER'S APPRENTICE

(Theme)

PAUL DUKAS

March tempo, in 1

SPRING
from THE FOUR SEASONS
(First Movement Theme)

ANTONIO VIVALDI

SICILIANO
from FLUTE SONATA NO. 2

HORN

JOHANN SEBASTIAN BACH

Andante

SKATERS WALTZ

HORN

ÉMILE WALDTEUFEL

SLEEPERS, AWAKE

from CANTATA 140

HORN

JOHANN SEBASTIAN BACH

SPINNING SONG

HORN

ALBERT ELLMENREICH

SWAN LAKE
(Theme)

HORN

PYOTR IL'YICH TCHAIKOVSKY

Moderately

SYMPHONY NO. 5
(First Movement Theme)

HORN

LUDWIG VAN BEETHOVEN

Allegro con brio

70

SYMPHONY NO. 1
(Fourth Movement Theme)

HORN

JOHANNES BRAHMS

SYMPHONY NO. 7
(Second Movement Theme)

LUDWIG VAN BEETHOVEN

SYMPHONY NO. 9

"From the New World"
(Second Movement Theme)

ANTONÍN DVOŘÁK

SYMPHONY NO. 40
(First Movement Theme)

HORN

WOLFGANG AMADEUS MOZART

SYMPHONY NO. 40
(Third Movement Theme)

HORN

WOLFGANG AMADEUS MOZART

Allegretto

TALES FROM THE VIENNA WOODS

HORN

JOHANN STRAUSS, JR.

Waltz tempo

TO A WILD ROSE
from WOODLAND SKETCHES

HORN

75

EDWARD MACDOWELL

Moderately, tenderly

SURPRISE SYMPHONY
(Symphony No. 94, Second Movement Theme)

HORN

FRANZ JOSEPH HAYDN

TRÄUMERAI
from SCENES FROM CHILDHOOD

ROBERT SCHUMANN

TRUMPET TUNE

HENRY PURCELL

Moderately

TRUMPET VOLUNTARY

(Prince of Denmark's March)

HORN

JEREMIAH CLARKE

Moderately

WILLIAM TELL OVERTURE
(Theme)

HORN

GIOACHINO ROSSINI

Allegro vivace

UNFINISHED SYMPHONY
(Symphony No. 8)
(First Movement Theme)

HORN

FRANZ SCHUBERT

Allegro moderato

WALTZ OF THE FLOWERS
from THE NUTCRACKER

PYOTR IL'YICH TCHAIKOVSKY

Waltz tempo

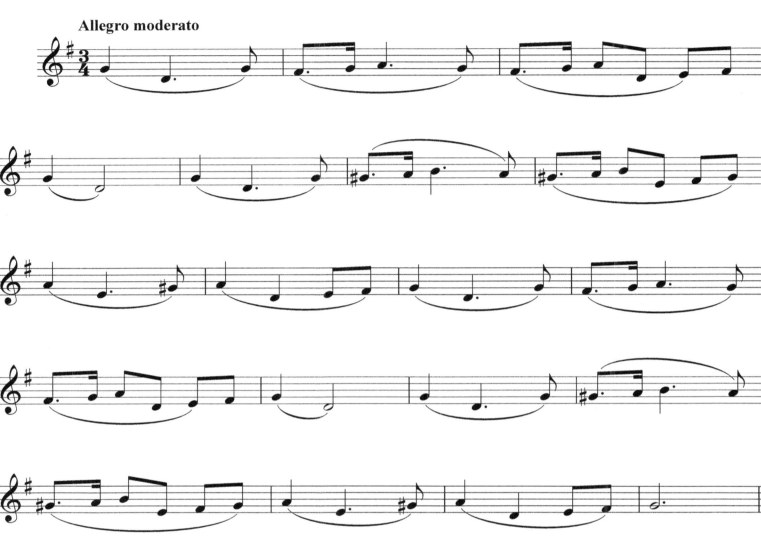

WALTZ IN C-SHARP MINOR, OP. 64, NO. 2

HORN

FRÉDÉRIC CHOPIN

Waltz tempo

TOREADOR SONG
from CARMEN

HORN

GEORGES BIZET

Allegro moderato

WEDDING MARCH
from A MIDSUMMER NIGHT'S DREAM

FELIX MENDELSSOHN

Allegro vivace

Fine

D.C. al Fine
(no repeat)

WHERE'ER YOU WALK
from SEMELE

HORN

GEORGE FRIDERIC HANDEL

Largo

THE WILD HORSEMAN
from ALBUM FOR THE YOUNG

ROBERT SCHUMANN

Lively

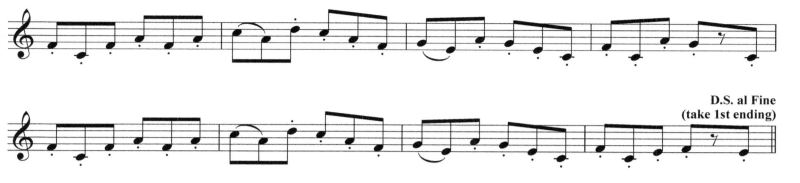

D.S. al Fine
(take 1st ending)

WINTER
from THE FOUR SEASONS
(Second Movement Theme)

ANTONIO VIVALDI

Largo

101 SONGS

BIG COLLECTIONS OF FAVORITE SONGS ARRANGED FOR SOLO INSTRUMENTALISTS.

101 BROADWAY SONGS

00154199	Flute	$15.99
00154200	Clarinet	$15.99
00154201	Alto Sax	$15.99
00154202	Tenor Sax	$16.99
00154203	Trumpet	$15.99
00154204	Horn	$15.99
00154205	Trombone	$15.99
00154206	Violin	$15.99

00154207 Viola...$15.99
00154208 Cello...$15.99

101 DISNEY SONGS

00244104	Flute	$17.99
00244106	Clarinet	$17.99
00244107	Alto Sax	$17.99
00244108	Tenor Sax	$17.99
00244109	Trumpet	$17.99
00244112	Horn	$17.99
00244120	Trombone	$17.99
00244121	Violin	$17.99

00244125 Viola...$17.99
00244126 Cello...$17.99

101 MOVIE HITS

00158087	Flute	$15
00158088	Clarinet	$15
00158089	Alto Sax	$15
00158090	Tenor Sax	$15
00158091	Trumpet	$15
00158092	Horn	$15
00158093	Trombone	$15
00158094	Violin	$15

00158095 Viola...$15
00158096 Cello...$15

101 CHRISTMAS SONGS

00278637	Flute	$15.99
00278638	Clarinet	$15.99
00278639	Alto Sax	$15.99
00278640	Tenor Sax	$15.99
00278641	Trumpet	$15.99
00278642	Horn	$14.99
00278643	Trombone	$15.99
00278644	Violin	$15.99

00278645 Viola...$15.99
00278646 Cello...$15.99

101 HIT SONGS

00194561	Flute	$17.99
00197182	Clarinet	$17.99
00197183	Alto Sax	$17.99
00197184	Tenor Sax	$17.99
00197185	Trumpet	$17.99
00197186	Horn	$17.99
00197187	Trombone	$17.99
00197188	Violin	$17.99

00197189 Viola...$17.99
00197190 Cello...$17.99

101 POPULAR SONGS

00224722	Flute	$17.
00224723	Clarinet	$17.
00224724	Alto Sax	$17.
00224725	Tenor Sax	$17.
00224726	Trumpet	$17
00224727	Horn	$17
00224728	Trombone	$17.
00224729	Violin	$17.

00224730 Viola...$17.
00224731 Cello...$17.

101 CLASSICAL THEMES

00155315	Flute	$15.99
00155317	Clarinet	$15.99
00155318	Alto Sax	$15.99
00155319	Tenor Sax	$15.99
00155320	Trumpet	$15.99
00155321	Horn	$15.99
00155322	Trombone	$15.99
00155323	Violin	$15.99

00155324 Viola...$15.99
00155325 Cello...$15.99

101 JAZZ SONGS

00146363	Flute	$15.99
00146364	Clarinet	$15.99
00146366	Alto Sax	$15.99
00146367	Tenor Sax	$15.99
00146368	Trumpet	$15.99
00146369	Horn	$14.99
00146370	Trombone	$15.99
00146371	Violin	$15.99

00146372 Viola...$15.99
00146373 Cello...$15.99

101 MOST BEAUTIFUL SONG

00291023	Flute	$16
00291041	Clarinet	$16
00291042	Alto Sax	$17
00291043	Tenor Sax	$17
00291044	Trumpet	$16
00291045	Horn	$16
00291046	Trombone	$16
00291047	Violin	$16

00291048 Viola...$16
00291049 Cello...$17

See complete song lists and sample pages at www.halleonard.com

HAL•LEONARD®
www.halleonard.com

Prices, contents and availability subject to change without notice.

HAL•LEONARD INSTRUMENTAL PLAY-ALONG

Your favorite songs are arranged just for solo instrumentalists with this outstanding series. Each book includes great full-accompaniment play-along audio so you can sound just like a pro!

Check out **halleonard.com** for songlists and more titles!

12 Pop Hits
12 songs
00261790	Flute	00261795	Horn
00261791	Clarinet	00261796	Trombone
00261792	Alto Sax	00261797	Violin
00261793	Tenor Sax	00261798	Viola
00261794	Trumpet	00261799	Cello

The Very Best of Bach
15 selections
00225371	Flute	00225376	Horn
00225372	Clarinet	00225377	Trombone
00225373	Alto Sax	00225378	Violin
00225374	Tenor Sax	00225379	Viola
00225375	Trumpet	00225380	Cello

The Beatles
15 songs
00225330	Flute	00225335	Horn
00225331	Clarinet	00225336	Trombone
00225332	Alto Sax	00225337	Violin
00225333	Tenor Sax	00225338	Viola
00225334	Trumpet	00225339	Cello

Chart Hits
12 songs
00146207	Flute	00146212	Horn
00146208	Clarinet	00146213	Trombone
00146209	Alto Sax	00146214	Violin
00146210	Tenor Sax	00146211	Trumpet
00146216	Cello		

Christmas Songs
12 songs
00146855	Flute	00146863	Horn
00146858	Clarinet	00146864	Trombone
00146859	Alto Sax	00146866	Violin
00146860	Tenor Sax	00146867	Viola
00146862	Trumpet	00146868	Cello

Contemporary Broadway
15 songs
00298704	Flute	00298709	Horn
00298705	Clarinet	00298710	Trombone
00298706	Alto Sax	00298711	Violin
00298707	Tenor Sax	00298712	Viola
00298708	Trumpet	00298713	Cello

Disney Movie Hits
12 songs
00841420	Flute	00841424	Horn
00841687	Oboe	00841425	Trombone
00841421	Clarinet	00841426	Violin
00841422	Alto Sax	00841427	Viola
00841686	Tenor Sax	00841428	Cello
00841423	Trumpet		

Prices, contents, and availability subject to change without notice.

Disney characters and artwork ™ & © 2021 Disney

Disney Solos
12 songs
00841404	Flute	00841506	Oboe
00841406	Alto Sax	00841409	Trumpet
00841407	Horn	00841410	Violin
00841411	Viola	00841412	Cello
00841405	Clarinet/Tenor Sax		
00841408	Trombone/Baritone		
00841553	Mallet Percussion		

Dixieland Favorites
15 songs
00268756	Flute	0068759	Trumpet
00268757	Clarinet	00268760	Trombone
00268758	Alto Sax		

Billie Eilish
9 songs
00345648	Flute	00345653	Horn
00345649	Clarinet	00345654	Trombone
00345650	Alto Sax	00345655	Violin
00345651	Tenor Sax	00345656	Viola
00345652	Trumpet	00345657	Cello

Favorite Movie Themes
13 songs
00841166	Flute	00841168	Trumpet
00841167	Clarinet	00841170	Trombone
00841169	Alto Sax	00841296	Violin

Gospel Hymns
15 songs
00194648	Flute	00194654	Trombone
00194649	Clarinet	00194655	Horn
00194650	Alto Sax	00194656	Viola
00194651	Tenor Sax	00194657	Cello
00194652	Trumpet		

Great Classical Themes
15 songs
00292727	Flute	00292733	Horn
00292728	Clarinet	00292735	Trombone
00292729	Alto Sax	00292736	Violin
00292730	Tenor Sax	00292737	Viola
00292732	Trumpet	00292738	Cello

The Greatest Showman
8 songs
00277389	Flute	00277394	Horn
00277390	Clarinet	00277395	Trombone
00277391	Alto Sax	00277396	Violin
00277392	Tenor Sax	00277397	Viola
00277393	Trumpet	00277398	Cello

Irish Favorites
31 songs
00842489	Flute	00842495	Trombone
00842490	Clarinet	00842496	Violin
00842491	Alto Sax	00842497	Viola
00842493	Trumpet	00842498	Cello
00842494	Horn		

Michael Jackson
11 songs
00119495	Flute	00119499	Trumpet
00119496	Clarinet	00119501	Trombone
00119497	Alto Sax	00119503	Violin
00119498	Tenor Sax	00119502	Accomp.

Jazz & Blues
14 songs
00841438	Flute	00841441	Trumpet
00841439	Clarinet	00841443	Trombone
00841440	Alto Sax	00841444	Violin
00841442	Tenor Sax		

Jazz Classics
12 songs
00151812	Flute	00151816	Trumpet
00151813	Clarinet	00151818	Trombone
00151814	Alto Sax	00151819	Violin
00151815	Tenor Sax	00151821	Cello

Les Misérables
13 songs
00842292	Flute	00842297	Horn
00842293	Clarinet	00842298	Trombone
00842294	Alto Sax	00842299	Violin
00842295	Tenor Sax	00842300	Viola
00842296	Trumpet	00842301	Cello

Metallica
12 songs
02501327	Flute	02502454	Horn
02501339	Clarinet	02501329	Trombone
02501332	Alto Sax	02501334	Violin
02501333	Tenor Sax	02501335	Viola
02501330	Trumpet	02501338	Cello

Motown Classics
15 songs
00842572	Flute	00842576	Trumpet
00842573	Clarinet	00842578	Trombone
00842574	Alto Sax	00842579	Violin
00842575	Tenor Sax		

Pirates of the Caribbean
16 songs
00842183	Flute	00842188	Horn
00842184	Clarinet	00842189	Trombone
00842185	Alto Sax	00842190	Violin
00842186	Tenor Sax	00842191	Viola
00842187	Trumpet	00842192	Cello

Queen
17 songs
00285402	Flute	00285407	Horn
00285403	Clarinet	00285408	Trombone
00285404	Alto Sax	00285409	Violin
00285405	Tenor Sax	00285410	Viola
00285406	Trumpet	00285411	Cello

Simple Songs
14 songs
00249081	Flute	00249087	Horn
00249093	Oboe	00249089	Trombone
00249082	Clarinet	00249090	Violin
00249083	Alto Sax	00249091	Viola
00249084	Tenor Sax	00249092	Cello
00249086	Trumpet	00249094	Mallets

Superhero Themes
14 songs
00363195	Flute	00363200	Horn
00363196	Clarinet	00363201	Trombone
00363197	Alto Sax	00363202	Violin
00363198	Tenor Sax	00363203	Viola
00363199	Trumpet	00363204	Cello

Star Wars
16 songs
00350900	Flute	00350907	Horn
00350913	Oboe	00350908	Trombone
00350903	Clarinet	00350909	Violin
00350904	Alto Sax	00350910	Viola
00350905	Tenor Sax	00350911	Cello
00350906	Trumpet	00350914	Mallet

Taylor Swift
15 songs
00842532	Flute	00842537	Horn
00842533	Clarinet	00842538	Trombone
00842534	Alto Sax	00842539	Violin
00842535	Tenor Sax	00842540	Viola
00842536	Trumpet	00842541	Cello

Video Game Music
13 songs
00283877	Flute	00283883	Horn
00283878	Clarinet	00283884	Trombone
00283879	Alto Sax	00283885	Violin
00283880	Tenor Sax	00283886	Viola
00283882	Trumpet	00283887	Cello

Wicked
13 songs
00842236	Flute	00842241	Horn
00842237	Clarinet	00842242	Trombone
00842238	Alto Sax	00842243	Violin
00842239	Tenor Sax	00842244	Viola
00842240	Trumpet	00842245	Cello

HAL•LEONARD®

Classical PLAY-ALONG

The Hal Leonard Classical Play-Along™ series will help you play great classical pieces. Listen to the full performance tracks to hear how the piece sounds with an orchestra, and then play along using the accompaniment tracks. The audio CD is playable on any CD player. For PC and Mac computer users, the CD is enhanced so you can adjust the recording to any tempo without changing pitch.

1. **MOZART:**
   FLUTE CONCERTO IN D MAJOR, K314
   Book/CD Pack
   00842341 Flute......................$12.99

2. **SAMMARTINI:**
   DESCANT (SOPRANO) RECORDER
   CONCERTO IN F MAJOR
   Book/CD Pack
   00842342 Soprano Recorder.............$12.99

3. **LOEILLET:**
   TREBLE (ALTO) RECORDER
   SONATA IN G MAJOR, OP.1, NO.3
   Book/CD Pack
   00842343 Alto Recorder................$12.99

4. **MOZART:**
   CLARINET CONCERTO IN A MAJOR, K622
   Book/CD Pack
   00842344 Clarinet.....................$12.99

6. **MOZART:**
   HORN CONCERTO IN D MAJOR, K412/514
   Book/CD Pack
   00842346 Horn.........................$12.99

7. **BACH:**
   VIOLIN CONCERTO IN A MINOR, BWV 1041
   Book/CD Pack
   00842347 Violin.......................$12.99

8. **TELEMANN:**
   VIOLA CONCERTO IN G MAJOR, TWV 51:G9
   Book/Online Audio
   00842348 Viola........................$12.99

9. **HAYDN:**
   CELLO CONCERTO IN C MAJOR, HOB.
   VIIB: 1
   Book/CD Pack
   00842349 Cello........................$12.99

10. **BACH:**
    PIANO CONCERTO IN F MINOR, BWV 1056
    Book/CD Pack
    00842350 Piano.......................$12.99

11. **PERGOLESI:**
    FLUTE CONCERTO IN G MAJOR
    Book/CD Pack
    00842351 Flute.......................$12.99

12. **BARRE:**
    DESCANT (SOPRANO) RECORDER
    SUITE NO. 9 "DEUXIEME LIVRE" G MAJOR
    Book/Online Audio
    00842352 Soprano Recorder............$12.99

14. **VON WEBER:**
    CLARINET CONCERTO NO. 1 IN F MINOR,
    OP. 73
    Book/CD Pack
    00842354 Clarinet....................$12.99

15. **MOZART:**
    VIOLIN CONCERTO IN G MAJOR, K216
    Book/CD Pack
    00842355 Violin......................$12.99

16. **BOCCHERINI:**
    CELLO CONCERTO IN B-FLAT MAJOR,
    G482
    Book/CD Pack
    00842356 Cello.......................$12.99

17. **MOZART:**
    PIANO CONCERTO IN C MAJOR, K467
    Book/CD Pack
    00842357 Piano.......................$12.99

18. **BACH:**
    FLUTE SONATA IN E-FLAT MAJOR,
    BWV 1031
    Book/CD Pack
    00842450 Flute.......................$12.99

19. **BRAHMS:**
    CLARINET SONATA IN F MINOR, OP. 120,
    NO. 1
    Book/CD Pack
    00842451 Clarinet....................$12.99

20. **BEETHOVEN:**
    TWO ROMANCES FOR VIOLIN,
    OP. 40 IN G & OP. 50 IN F
    Book/CD Pack
    00842452 Violin......................$12.99

21. **MOZART:**
    PIANO CONCERTO IN D MINOR, K466
    Book/CD Pack
    00842453 Piano.......................$12.99

Prices, content, and availability subject to change without notice.

www.halleonard.com

0